Teddy Ruxpin Sings Love Songs

There's nothing like a love song to tell someone how you feel.

Vocal Interpretation by:
Phil Baron

Illustrated by:

Russell Hicks
Theresa Mazurek
Douglas McCarthy
Allyn Conley-Gorniak
Lorann Downer

Rivka
Fay Whitemountain
Suzanne Lewis
Lisa Souza

W•W
WORLDS OF WONDER™

Worlds of Wonder, Inc. is the exclusive licensee, manufacturer and distributor of the World of Teddy Ruxpin toys. "The World of Teddy Ruxpin" and "Teddy Ruxpin" are trademarks of Alchemy II, Inc., Chatsworth, CA. The symbol W•W and "Worlds of Wonder" are trademarks of Worlds of Wonder, Inc., Fremont, California.

Grubby® Newton Gimmick™ Princess Aruzia™ Leota™ Wooly What's-It™ Prince Arin™ Fobs®

"It Might As Well Be Spring"

I'm as restless as a willow in a windstorm.
I'm as jumpy as a puppet on a string.
I'd say that I had spring fever,
But I know it isn't spring.

I am starry-eyed and vaguely discontented,
Like a nightingale without a song to sing.
Oh, why should I have spring fever
When it isn't even spring?

Page 1

I keep wishing I were somewhere else,
Walking down a strange new street,
Hearing words that I have never heard
From a girl I've yet to meet.

I'm as busy as a spider spinning daydreams.
I'm as giddy as a baby on a swing.
I haven't seen a crocus or a rosebud
Or a robin on the wing.

But I feel so gay
In a melancholy way,
That it might as well be spring.
It might as well be spring.

Words by Oscar Hammerstein II. Music by Richard Rodgers.

"When I Fall In Love"

When I fall in love
It will be forever
Or I'll never fall in love.
In a restless world like this is,
Love is ended before it's begun,
And too many moonlight kisses
Seem to cool in the warmth
   of the sun.

When I give my heart
It will be completely
Or I'll never give my heart.
And the moment I can feel that
You feel that way, too,
Is when I fall in love with you.

Words by Edward Heyman. Music by Victor Young.
© 1952 Chappell and Co., Inc./Intersong–U.S.A., Inc. Used by permission.

"I Only Have Eyes For You"

My love must be a kind of blind love,
I can't see anyone but you.

Are the stars out tonight?
I don't know if it's cloudy or bright,
'Cause I only have eyes for you, dear.

The moon may be high,
But I can't see a thing in the sky,
'Cause I only have eyes for you.

I don't know if we're in a garden
Or on a crowded avenue.
You are here, so am I.
Maybe millions of people go by.
But they all disappear from view,
And I only have eyes for you.

"Let Me Call You Sweetheart"

Chorus

Let me call you sweetheart.
I'm in love with you.
Let me hear you whisper
That you love me, too.
Keep the love-light glowing
In your eyes so true.
Let me call you sweetheart.
I'm in love with you.

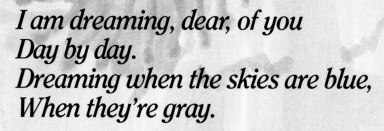

I am dreaming, dear, of you
Day by day.
Dreaming when the skies are blue,
When they're gray.

When the silv'ry moonlight gleams
Still I wander on in dreams
In a land of love, it seems
Just with you.

Repeat Chorus

Words by Beth Slater Whitson. Music by Leo Friedman.
This arrangement © 1986 Rillonia Music Corp. Used by permission. All rights reserved.

"Dream A Little Dream Of Me"

Stars shining bright above you,
Night breezes seem to whisper,
  "I love you,"
Birds singing in the sycamore
  tree,
Dream a little dream of me.

Say "night-ie-night" and kiss me,
Just hold me tight and tell me
  you'll miss me.
While I'm alone and blue as
  can be,
Dream a little dream
  of me.

Stars fading, but I linger on, dear,
Still craving your kiss.
I'm longing to linger till dawn, dear,
Just saying this:

Sweet dreams till sunbeams find you,
Sweet dreams that leave all worries
  behind you.
      But in your dreams whatever
      they be,
          Dream a little dream of me.

"Someone To Watch Over Me"

There's a saying old says that love is blind,
Still we're often told, "Seek and ye shall find."
So I'm going to seek a certain gal I've had
   in mind.

Looking everywhere, haven't found her yet.
She's the big affair I cannot forget.
Only girl I ever think of with regret.

I'd like to add her initial to my monogram.
Tell me, where is the shepherd for this
   lost lamb?

There's a somebody I'm longing to see.
I hope that she turns out to be
Someone who'll watch over me.

I'm a little lamb who's lost in the wood.
I know I could always be good
To one who'll watch over me.

Although I may not be the man some
Girls think of as handsome.
To my heart she carries the key.

Won't you tell her please
To put on some speed,
Follow my lead,
Oh, how I need
Someone to watch over me.